Illustrator:
Jose L. Tapia

Editor:
Janet Cain, M. Ed.

Editorial Project Manager:
Ina Massler Levin, M.A.

Editor in Chief:
Sharon Coan, M.S. Ed.

Art Director:
Elayne Roberts

Associate Designer:
Denise Bauer

Cover Artists:
Sue Fullam
Marc Kazlauskas

Product Manager:
Phil Garcia

Imaging:
James Edward Grace
Ralph Olmedo, Jr.

Publishers:
Rachelle Cracchiolo, M.S. Ed.
Mary Dupuy Smith, M.S. Ed.

Learning Center Activities

Science

K-2

Author:

Deborah M. Candelora, M.S.E.

Teacher Created Materials, Inc.
P.O. Box 1040
Huntington Beach, CA   92647
ISBN-1-57690-072-X

©1996 Teacher Created Materials, Inc.   Made in U.S.A.

Table of Contents

Introduction

Hands-on science activities give students opportunities to explore the world around them and make connections with the things they experience. Because students are naturally curious they find science exciting to study. Teachers are facilitators, guiding students through the investigative process, showing them how to document their data and observations, and helping them interpret and apply what they have learned.

There are differing opinions about whether science should be taught from textbooks or through the use of experiments. Some teachers prefer textbooks because of time constraints. It is easier to read from books than to set up and do experiments. The use of science centers capitalizes on the benefits of both types of instruction. Textbooks can be used for whole class instruction while centers can provide students with opportunities to experience the excitement of hands-on investigations.

One concern teachers sometimes have about teaching hands-on science is that they feel they do not have sufficient training in this area. In reality, having a limited background is less likely to affect instruction that takes place using experiments. The reason for this is that students focus on learning from their observations, rather than accepting what are generally considered to be the "facts" of science. If students have questions about something they have observed, it is up to them, not the teacher, to use further experimentation as they attempt to understand and explain what happened.

Teachers often worry that something will go wrong during an experiment and not all students will achieve the expected results. This can and often does happen. However, you will find that students often learn more from their mistakes than they do from having "perfect" results. By discussing the differences among students' observations, your class will get a much deeper understanding of the principles involved. They should also realize that conducting the same experiment does not guarantee the same results, making one answer just as good as another. Since there is less pressure on students to find the one and only correct answer, their enjoyment of science will increase and their ability as problem solvers will improve.

The experiments in *Learning Center Activities: Science* are designed to teach many facets of science. Students develop a better understanding of the basic scientific principles involved, increase their powers of observation, and become more aware of the world around them. Students also become familiar with the scientific process, learn to use various pieces of scientific equipment, and get acquainted with some techniques for collecting and analyzing data.

Science experiments are truly cross-curricular activities. Many involve math skills, such as measurement and problem solving. All involve reading and writing skills. As students conduct their experiments, they can learn a variety of social skills, such as cooperation, as well as work and study habits, such as self-discipline.

How to Use This Book

This book contains twenty-one experiments in the following six areas of science: earth science, structures and mechanics, life science, electricity and magnetism, sound, and simple chemistry. These experiments are designed to be done by individuals or pairs of students in grades K-2. Experiments take approximately 10-15 minutes each, making them easy to fit into your daily schedule. They can be done in any order so you can correlate them with your curriculum.

The introductory sections of this book offer general guidance on setting up and managing a Science Center in your classroom. This information includes a complete list of the materials (pages 9–10) required for all of the activities and some suggestions for where to obtain them. Teacher pages for each experiment provide background on the scientific principles involved, notes on how to prepare students for the activity, a list of materials needed, directions for how to set up the center, and suggested follow-up activities.

The teacher pages are followed by student activity pages, or Lab Worksheets. These are designed to be reproduced for students. They should be used to guide students through the experiments and help them document their work. Each experiment comes with Lab Worksheets at two different academic levels, A and B. The Lab Worksheets for Level B are intended for higher grades or more advanced students in lower grades. These pages are written at a higher reading level, require more writing on the part of students, and have more challenging questions and procedures.

All student activity pages are divided into four parts: the hypothesis, materials, procedure, and conclusion. To make it simpler and less intimidating, these sections are called "Ask Yourself," "What You Need," "What You Do," and "What You Learned." You may wish to introduce the technical terms and relate them as shown below.

Since Levels A and B fundamentally cover the same concepts, you can either select the one that is most appropriate for your class or you may use both. If you have a class with a broad range of abilities, make use of the dual-level approach by assigning the activity pages based on each student's abilities. This allows all of the students in your class to participate in and be challenged by the experiments in the Science Center.

Ask Yourself	Hypothesis
What You Need	Materials
What You Do	Procedure
What You Learned	Conclusion

Managing a Science Center

There are four phases to each of the 21 hands-on activities described in this book:

1. Preparing the Science Center for the experiment.

2. Introducing the experiment to students.

3. Acting as a facilitator as students do the experiment.

4. Closing the activity by summarizing students' results.

Preparation

Set out the materials for an experiment before students start taking turns in the Science Center. Each student should go to the center with a copy of the appropriate Lab Worksheet and a pencil. Students should check off each material listed on the worksheet once they confirm that it is available in the center. Likewise, they should check off each step of the procedure after they have completed it. They should be sure to clean up after themselves, leaving the center in the same condition it was in when they arrived.

Introduction

The experiments are not intended to teach the basic scientific principles involved, rather to reinforce and extend them. Therefore, you will need to spend some time introducing your class to each subject prior to engaging students in an actual experiment. This can be done in a variety of ways such as reading a book, watching a movie or video tape, or discussing what students already know. The specific concepts that you need to address are described on the lesson page for each experiment. You might also want to talk about the branch of science and types of scientific careers that are associated with each experiment.

Read over the experiment with your class. This is an excellent opportunity for a discussion about what students already know, questions they might have, or specific procedures you want them to follow for getting supplies or cleaning up. If there are some specific procedures that are new or seem difficult, you should demonstrate them. Be sure you do not demonstrate the entire experiment since this will make it too easy for students to simply copy what they saw you do, rather than reading the directions and following the step-by-step procedure by themselves.

Lab Worksheets (Level A and Level B) are provided for each experiment. Both levels start by asking students to think about a question. Since it is difficult and time consuming for the younger students to write, the questions on the Level A worksheets may be better addressed in a class discussion rather than having students write their answers. Level A worksheets can also be used by students with special needs. Students using Level B worksheets should write their hypotheses. You may choose to have them do this immediately following the class discussion or while waiting for their turns in the Science Center.

Consider having two or three students work together. Exchanging ideas is an important part of the scientific process. If you do choose this team approach, encourage each member to actively participate in the experiment. Each student should be required to fill out his or her own copy of the Lab Worksheet.

Managing a Science Center (cont.)

Acting as Facilitator

Each experiment should be available in the Science Center for no more than two weeks. This allows the introduction of the topic to be fresh in students' minds while they are performing the experiment, and it is a short enough time period that they will still be able to recall their work during the closing discussion.

While students are performing the experiments, keep an eye on them to see that they are following the procedures and writing down their observations as needed. Warn them about safety concerns such as glass bottles that are too near the edge of the desk or table, spilled water, or safety goggles that are not being worn properly. As your class gets used to the general Science Center procedures, they will require fewer reminders from you.

When students come to you with questions, encourage them to find answers for themselves. Try to respond in a way that makes them responsible for answering their own questions. Some examples follow.

What do you think? and *What does your partner or group think?*

What did you do already? and *What do you need to do next?*

What did you observe?

How can you find out? or *What can you do to find out?*

When students ask if they got the right answers, remind them that there are no right answers. It is important that they learn to record and understand their own observations. If a student is concerned that she or he has gotten an answer that is different from other students' answers, suggest that she or he repeat the experiment. If the student gets the same results, she or he will have more confidence in his or her observations. If the student gets new results, she or he may be able to discover why there was a difference.

Closure

Each hands-on activity should be concluded with a class review and discussion of students' results and observations. This exchange of information and comparison of results is an important part of the scientific process. It also reinforces what students have learned and allows the inevitable discrepancies in their findings to be analyzed and understood.

If different students make seemingly conflicting observations, there are a few ways to pursue it. First, make it clear that no student is wrong. Ask each student (or the one that has different results than the majority of the class) to repeat the experiment to see if she or he gets the same results Ask another student to watch, paying particular attention to the procedure that is used. Often the differing results are because of variations in the procedure.

Assessment of student performance on these activities should be based on the completeness and clarity of their answers on their Lab Worksheets, their behavior during the experiment, and their participation in class discussions rather than on whether or not they got the "right answer."

Setting Up a Science Center

Location

Here are some suggested guidelines to keep in mind as you set up your Science Center.

1. A student desk or small table provides a sufficient work area. The experiments are intentionally designed to be exciting, so you may want to put the center in a corner where it will not disturb other students.

2. Display the Science Center sign (page 11) and/or other scientific decorations.

3. Hands-on science activities can be messy. Suggestions have been provided to help minimize the mess. However, you should still set up the center in a place where there is nothing nearby or underneath that can be damaged if an accident occurs.

4. You will need a place to keep the Science Center materials. However, this does not need to be near the center. You can store all of the science materials elsewhere in your classroom. Set out the materials needed for a specific activity on the day(s) the class will be performing that experiment.

5. You will need some room around the Science Center for things such as a trash can, bucket, and bottle of water. Other specific items are described for each experiment.

Materials

Many of the materials used in the Science Center are intentionally selected to be everyday items that students may be able to find at home. This not only helps to reduce expenses but encourages students to extend their investigations outside of the classroom.

In some cases, special pieces of equipment are needed. These are simple, inexpensive items that typically can be purchased at educational toy stores, hobby shops, or through educational supply companies such as those listed below.

Edmund Scientific Company
101 East Gloucester Pike
Barrington, NJ 08007-9897
1-609-547-8880

Delta Education, Inc.
Hands-On Science K-8
Nashua, NH 03061-3000
1-800-442-5444

Cuisenaire Co. of America, Inc.
10 Bank Street
White Plains, NY 10602-5026
1-800-237-0338

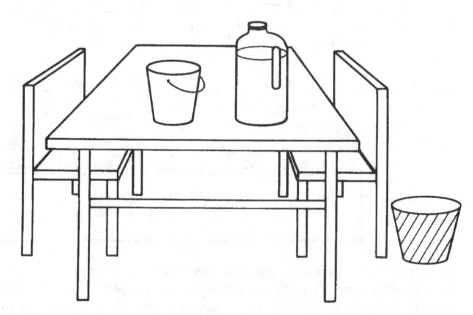

Setting Up a Science Center (cont.)

Materials (cont.)

You may wish to obtain materials prior to having students do each experiment, or you can purchase the materials needed for all of the experiments before students begin working on any of them. Keep in mind that if you have to order some items from a catalog, they may take a few weeks to arrive. Also, a few of the items may need some simple preparations before they can be used. These are described in the lesson pages for those particular experiments.

You may wish to ask parent volunteers to help collect and prepare the materials. They may be able to contribute many of the items. Inviting the parents to see the center in action is an easy way to thank them for their contributions.

A complete listing of all of the materials needed for a class of 24 students to perform every experiment described in this book appears on pages 9-10. The materials are divided into groups according to where you will most likely be able to purchase them. Most of the items can be obtained from more than one source. This list does not include any extras, so you may wish to get additional quantities of those items that might get lost or that are considered consumable. For storage purposes, you can keep all of the materials together in a box. A photocopier paper box works well for this.

Some of the items are used in more than one experiment. As a result, you may wish to keep the equipment for each activity separate. If this is the case, you will need to obtain duplicate items so there are sufficient supplies in each box. The lesson page for each experiment lists the items needed for that particular activity. Be sure to label the outside of the box with the name of the experiment and a list of the materials that are enclosed. This will make it easy to check and refurbish the equipment in the future.

DISSECTING DIRT

Some of the experiments require the use of water or other liquids. If you do not have a sink close to the Science Center, you can use clean plastic milk bottles to hold water. Fill the bottles only part way to make them easier for students to manage. Have students dispose of the liquids by pouring them into a bucket after completing the experiment. Then you can empty the bucket at the end of the day.

8

Materials List

The materials listed below and on page 10 are enough for a class of 24 students. Adjust the amounts according to the number of students in your class.

Grocery Store
- ❏ 24 plastic straws
- ❏ salt in a shaker
- ❏ pepper in a shaker
- ❏ 1 small bottle of dish detergent (You only need a few drops.)
- ❏ 1 small bottle of cooking oil (You only need a few drops.)
- ❏ 1 box of toothpicks
- ❏ 1 box of table salt
- ❏ 1 gallon (3.79 L) of white vinegar
- ❏ 1 disposable, clear plastic 8-ounce (250 mL) tumbler
- ❏ 72 paper cups, 3-ounce (90 mL) size
- ❏ 24 paper cups, 5-ounce (150 mL) size
- ❏ 24 paper cups, 8-ounce (250 mL) size
- ❏ 24 paper cups, 12-ounce (360 mL) size

Hardware Store
- ❏ 100 feet (30 m) of butcher twine or thin string
- ❏ 1 pair of safety goggles for each student working in the center
- ❏ 1 roll of masking tape
- ❏ 2 D-cell (flashlight) batteries
- ❏ 2 blocks, 3" (8 cm) long pieces of a 2" x 4" (5 cm x 10 cm)
- ❏ 1 fat wedge, 2" x 4" (5 cm x 10 cm) cut at a 60° angle
- ❏ 1 thin wedge
- ❏ 1 high intensity flashlight

Educational Toy Store
- ❏ 10 plastic "bugs"
- ❏ 1 magnet
- ❏ 1 magnifying glass or 30X hand-held microscope (Get a spare bulb and batteries.)
- ❏ 1 tornado tube
- ❏ 6 sticks of modeling clay
- ❏ 1 rattleback
- ❏ 24 play dollar bills, approximately the size of a real dollar bill

Materials List (cont.)

Discount Department Store

- ❏ 1 bowl or saucer, approximately 5" (13 cm) wide and 1-2" (2.5-5 cm) deep
- ❏ 1 funnel
- ❏ 1 metal teaspoon (5 mL)
- ❏ 1 bowl, 2 quart (1.9 L) size
- ❏ 1 bowl, 4-8 quart (3.8-7.6 L) size
- ❏ 1 stop watch or a clock with a second hand
- ❏ 2 flat fishing sinkers, 1-ounce (28 grams) size
- ❏ 2 flat fishing sinkers, 2-ounce (56 grams) size
- ❏ 2 flat fishing sinkers, ½-ounce (14 grams) size
- ❏ a bucket, if a sink is not readily available

General Classroom Supplies

- ❏ an assortment of small objects (See "Mystery Cans," "Magical Magnets," and "Go With the Flow" for specific lists.)
- ❏ 1 box of eight crayons
- ❏ 1 rubber band large enough to fit around the 4-8 quart (3.8-7.6 L) bowl
- ❏ 1 box of paper clips
- ❏ 1 hexagonal pencil
- ❏ 1 wooden, 12" (30 cm) ruler that is thick enough not to bend
- ❏ water (This can be stored in a plastic milk or juice container.)
- ❏ scrap paper
- ❏ paper towels

Household Items

- ❏ 10 plastic containers and lids from 35 mm film
- ❏ 1 side of a plastic grocery bag
- ❏ 1 small, empty food can, approximately 8-ounce (250 mL) size
- ❏ 3 identical 12-16 ounce (360-500 mL) glass soft drink bottles with lids
- ❏ 2 plastic 1-liter (1 quart) soda bottles
- ❏ 4 plastic squeeze bottles from dish detergent or shampoo with tops (Be sure the bottles are rinsed thoroughly.)
- ❏ 1 string of miniature Christmas tree lights (The lights do not need to work.)
- ❏ 1-2 old bath towels
- ❏ 10 quarters or flat washers of equivalent size
- ❏ 48 dirty pennies
- ❏ 1 clothes pin
- ❏ 2 types of dirt, approximately 3 cups (750 mL) of each
- ❏ 12 leaves (Collect these when they are needed so they do not dry out.)

SCIENCE CENTER

Rattlebacks

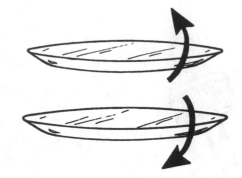

Background

Ordinary stones that are collected from a babbling brook can have interesting physical and scientific properties. Rattlebacks are stones of a particular shape that causes them to spin in only one direction. If you spin them in the other direction, they will quickly stop and reverse their spin. Rattlebacks occur naturally when stones are sculpted by the running water in a stream or river.

Objectives

- To reinforce the concept of erosion and the power of water to shape rock.
- To help students contrast and compare two events.

Student Instruction

This is an excellent lab for students to start with because it is simple, fun, and encourages their natural curiosity. Introduce your class to erosion and how rocks are sculpted by water. For students working on Lab Worksheet — Level A (page 13), review left and right. For those working on Level B (page 14), review the meanings of *clockwise* and *counterclockwise*.

Center Preparation

Materials: 1 rattleback

Directions: For this lab, you must buy a rattleback. These can be purchased in many educational toy stores, or they can be ordered from educational supply catalogs. No other equipment or preparation is needed.

Follow-Up Activities

Ask students to determine why this stone is called a *rattleback*. Try spinning the rattleback yourself. You will see that when you spin it clockwise, it stops, rattles up and down, and then turns back.

If you have access to a rock tumbler, set it up in your class. Tumble some rocks for students to show how water shapes the rocks. Take out two or three rocks at each stage of the tumbling so that the class can see the changes that are occurring. If you do not have access to a rock tumbler, you can purchase a few inexpensive polished stones at educational toy stores or hobby shops and compare them to some rough pebbles.

If your rattleback is clear plastic, see if your class has noticed that it can also serve as a magnifying glass.

Encourage students to give examples of how moving water has caused erosion at your school or in your community.

Name: _____ Date: _____

Rattlebacks

Lab Worksheet — Level A

Ask Yourself

Can I make the rattleback spin to the left? Can I make it spin to the right?

What You Need

_____ 1 rattleback

What You Do

_____ 1. Put the rattleback in **Box A** with the flat side up.

Box A

_____ 2. Spin the rattleback to the left, the way the arrow points.

_____ 3. Put the rattleback in **Box B** with the flat side up.

Box B

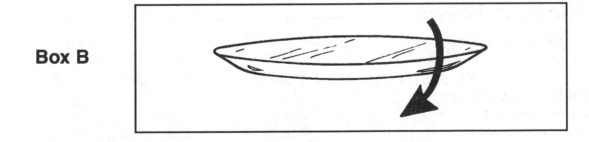

_____ 4. Spin the rattleback to the right, the way the arrow points.

What You Learned

Did the rattleback spin better in Box A or Box B?

_____ **Box A**   _____ **Box B**

Name: _____   Date: _____

Rattlebacks
Lab Worksheet — Level B

Ask Yourself

Will the rattleback spin the same in both directions (clockwise and counterclockwise)?

_____

What You Need

____   1 rattleback

What You Do

____   1. Place the rattleback with the flat side up on a table.

____   2. Try spinning the rattleback clockwise. What happens?

_____

____   3. Now try spinning the rattleback counterclockwise. What happens?

_____

____   4. With your finger, push one end of the rattleback down to the table.

____   5. Quickly let it go. What happens?

_____

What You Learned

Did the rattleback spin the same in both directions (clockwise and counterclockwise)?

_____

Can you figure out how rattlebacks got their name? Explain your answer.

_____

_____

Dissecting Dirt

Background

Every day we step on dirt without noticing it. Actually, dirt is not a single substance but is made up of several components, including small pieces of rocks and organic material.

There are many different types of sand and dirt. Each is made up of a different combination of materials.

Objectives

- To reveal that dirt is primarily made up of small pieces of rock.
- To help students realize the complexity of the natural world and that something as mundane as dirt can be fascinating.

Student Instruction

Explain that in your neighborhood, you might find reddish-brown soil that is rich in iron, hard black clay that turns into a quagmire when it rains, tan beach sand, or dark loamy garden soil. Have students obtain samples of different types of "dirt" from the community. Have students observe the differences in color, texture, etc., among the samples. Talk about why they think each one is different. Ask why different types of dirt might be better for different purposes such as growing crops.

Decide whether students will use a magnifying glass or a 30X microscope. Show students how to use the equipment you have chosen. Then model for them how to fill out the table in which they will record their results.

Center Preparation

Materials: 2 kinds of dirt, such as sand and garden soil, approximately 3 cups (750 mL) of each; 1 box of toothpicks; 1 magnifying glass or 30X microscope; scrap paper, preferably white; trash can

Directions: Obtain two containers, preferably with lids for storage. Place a different type of dirt in each container. Have a box of toothpicks available. **Helpful Hint:** You may want to hand out the toothpicks one at a time so students are not tempted to play with the whole box. Provide some scrap paper for students to place underneath their dirt samples. This will make cleanup easier. Be sure to put a trash can near the center. Place a magnifying glass or 30X hand-held microscope in the center. Inexpensive microscopes can usually be purchased from stores that sell educational toys. These microscopes provide a much better view of the dirt, but they may be difficult for very young students to use since they are monocular and require focusing.

Follow-Up Activities

Get several sizes of gravel and sand to demonstrate how rocks get progressively smaller until they become dirt. Discuss how different types of erosion help create dirt. Have students look for examples of erosion on the school grounds.

Name: _____ Date: _____

Dissecting Dirt

Lab Worksheet — Level A

Ask Yourself

What is dirt made of?

What You Need

_____ 1 sample of dirt

_____ 1 magnifying glass or microscope

_____ 1 toothpick

_____ 1 piece of paper

What You Do

_____ 1. Put your dirt on the paper.

_____ 2. Look at it through the magnifying glass or microscope.

_____ 3. Use the toothpick to spread it around.

_____ 4. You may see rocks, bits of plants or twigs, or even an insect or animal. Count how many different types of things you see in the dirt.

_____ 5. When you are finished, throw away your dirt sample.

What You Learned

How many different types of things were in the dirt? _____

_____

Name: _____ Date: _____

Dissecting Dirt
Lab Worksheet — Level B

Ask Yourself

What is dirt made of?_____

_____

What You Need

_____ 2 samples of dirt, A and B

_____ 1 magnifying glass or microscope

_____ 1 toothpick

_____ 1 piece of paper

What You Do

_____ 1. Put a small amount of dirt from Sample A on the paper.

_____ 2. Look at it through the magnifying glass or microscope. Use the toothpick to spread it around.

_____ 3. You may see rocks, bits of plants or twigs, or even part of an animal. On the chart below, write down how many of each you find.

_____ 4. Throw away your dirt from Sample A.

_____ 5. Now place a small amount of dirt from Sample B on the paper.

_____ 6. Repeat Steps 2-4 for Sample B. Be sure to use the chart to write down what you find.

	How Many?		
	Rocks	**Plant Parts**	**Animals**
Dirt Sample A			
Dirt Sample B			

What You Learned

Dirt is mostly made of_____ .

What is different about the two types of dirt? _____

_____

Tornadoes

Background

Although the exact causes of tornadoes are not yet understood, scientists know that they form when the strong updrafts (upward winds) of thunderstorms are combined with cross current winds that create twisting motions. We can simulate this using water instead of air, gravity instead of a thunderstorm, and by manually applying the twisting motion. The resulting "tornado" does not have the destructive power of its larger cousins, but it can be just as fascinating to watch.

Objectives

- To help students better understand tornadoes and storms.

- To introduce the concept of a simulation.

Student Instruction

Introduce tornadoes, cyclones, and other types of storms. Talk about how warm air rises and cold air sinks. Emphasize that the winds in tornadoes spin. Students will need to make use of the vertical and spinning motions to make their tornadoes.

Since tornadoes can be terribly destructive forces, they might seem frightening to some students. If you live in an area that is prone to tornadoes, you might want to review safety precautions and discuss the latest prediction capabilities of meteorologists.

Show your class how to use a funnel. Explain the routine you want students to follow for handling water and cleaning up the inevitable spills.

Center Preparation

Materials: 1 tornado tube, 2 one-liter (1.06 quart) plastic soda bottles, 1 funnel, water

Directions: For younger students, you might want to have the plastic bottles and tornado tube already assembled. A funnel will help older students fill the bottle with a minimum of spills. **Helpful Hint:** Put an old bath towel over the desk or table you are using for the Science Center. This will help absorb spilled water.

Follow-Up Activities

Ask students to see if they can make the tornado spin in either direction.

Compare the size, speed, and characteristics of hurricanes and tornadoes.

Throughout the school year, have students mark maps to show where hurricanes and tornadoes occur. Challenge them to track the movement of the hurricanes using latitude and longitude.

Invite students to do research to learn about the area of the United States called *Tornado Alley*.

Name: _____ Date: _____

Tornadoes

Lab Worksheet — Level A

Ask Yourself

Can I make a tornado in a bottle?

What You Need

_____ 1 tornado tube

_____ 1 funnel

_____ 2 bottles

_____ Water

What You Do

_____ 1. Use the funnel to pour water in one bottle until it is half full.

_____ 2. Screw the tornado tube onto the top of the bottle.

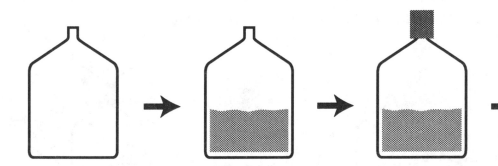

_____ 3. Screw the other bottle on top of the tornado tube.

_____ 4. Turn the bottles upside down.

_____ 5. Try to make a tornado by swirling the water.

What You Learned

Did you make a tornado?

_____ Yes _____ No

Name: _____ Date: _____

Tornadoes

Lab Worksheet — Level B

Ask Yourself

Can I make a tornado in a bottle? _____

_____

What You Need

_____ 1 tornado tube

_____ 1 funnel

_____ 2 bottles

_____ Water

What You Do

_____ 1. Use the funnel to pour water into one bottle until it is half full.

_____ 2. Screw the tornado tube onto the top of the bottle.

_____ 3. Screw the other bottle on top of the tornado tube.

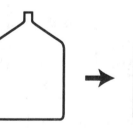 

_____ 4. Turn the bottles upside down.

_____ 5. Try to make a tornado by swirling the water.

What You Learned

Remember what you learned about tornadoes. What two motions were needed to make a tornado?_____

_____

_____

Over the Rainbow

Background

It takes both rain and sunshine to make a rainbow. When sunlight passes through a raindrop, it is split into all of its component colors. Each one is refracted, or bent, at a different angle, resulting in a rainbow. The raindrop acts just like a prism.

Objectives

- To learn that both light and water are required to make a rainbow.
- To introduce the concept of a model.

Student Instruction

Make sure students know the colors red, orange, yellow, green, blue, and purple. Show them how to use the flashlight. Ask students if they have ever seen a rainbow. See if they remember the colors that were in it and the order of the colors.

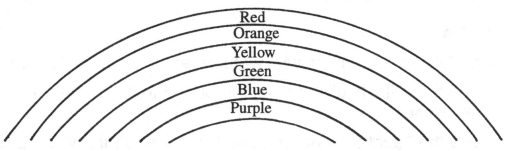

Center Preparation

Materials: 1 clear, 8 oz. (225 g) plastic cup; 1 high intensity flashlight with batteries; scrap paper; red, orange, yellow, green, blue, and purple crayons or markers

You can purchase the flashlight at any hardware store. Be sure to select one that is labeled *high intensity*. These have the light beam more tightly focused and will make a brighter rainbow.

Directions: Students will need to hang up white paper to use as a projection screen. If your Science Center is next to a wall, you can tape the paper to this. If not, allow them to attach the paper to a box or a large, hardback book standing on its end.

Finally, students will need a bottle of water and a set of crayons or markers that are the colors red, orange, yellow, green, blue, and purple. For younger students, you should fill the glass with water ahead of time. **Helpful Hints:** Cover the work area with an old bath towel to soak up spills, and have some paper towels handy to dry the floor if necessary.

Follow-Up Activities

Demonstrate how to make a rainbow with a prism. Verify that the colors appear in the same sequence that they did in this experiment.

Explain the significance that rainbows have in different cultures.

Earth Science

Name: _____ Date: _____

Over the Rainbow

Lab Worksheet — Level A

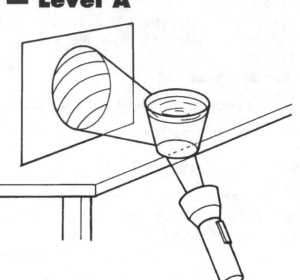

Ask Yourself

How can I make a rainbow?

What You Need

_____ White paper

_____ 1 plastic cup with water

_____ 1 flashlight

_____ Crayons or markers: blue, yellow, green, red, purple, orange

What You Do

_____ 1. Carefully put the glass with water near the edge of the desk or table.

_____ 2. Turn on the flashlight. Shine it through the glass of water toward the white paper.

_____ 3. Move the flashlight until you see a rainbow on the white paper.

_____ 4. In the box shown below, draw a picture of your rainbow. Be sure to place the bands of color in the order that you see them.

What You Learned

Draw a line from what you used in this experiment to what nature uses to make rainbows:

Water   Sun

Flashlight   Rain

Name: _____ Date: _____

Over the Rainbow

Lab Worksheet — Level B

Ask Yourself

How can I make a rainbow? _____

What You Need

_____ White paper

_____ 1 plastic cup

_____ Water

_____ 1 flashlight

_____ Crayons or markers: blue, yellow, green, red, purple, orange

What You Do

_____ 1. Fill the glass halfway with water.

_____ 2. Carefully put the glass near the edge of the desk or table.

_____ 3. Turn on the flashlight. Shine it through the glass of water toward the white paper.

_____ 4. Move the flashlight around until you see a rainbow on the white paper.

_____ 5. Draw your rainbow on the back of this paper. Use the same order of colors in your drawing that you saw in your rainbow.

What You Learned

When creating a rainbow, what does nature use instead of a cup of water and a flashlight?_____

In what order do the colors blue, red, yellow, purple, green, and orange appear in a rainbow?

Order	Color
Inner band	
Outer band	

Seesaw Science

Background

Science is everywhere. Even a playground is full of scientific principles. A seesaw is nothing more than a simple lever to which the principles of mechanics can be applied in order to have an enjoyable ride. The object the lever pivots on is called the fulcrum. If the load, or weight, on each side of the fulcrum is equal, the lever will balance. If the load on one end is greater than the load on the opposite end, the heavier end will sink. You can rebalance the lever by moving the fulcrum closer to the heavier load in one of two ways: either keep the load at the end of the lever and slide the fulcrum so that it is no longer in the center of the lever, or leave the fulcrum in the center of the lever and slide the load toward it so that the load is no longer at the end of the lever.

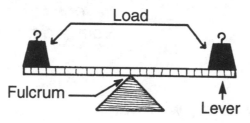

Objectives

- To help students gain a basic understanding of how levers operate and the meaning of the term *balance*.
- To learn how to document observations with a sketch or diagram.

Student Instruction

Find out how many students have been on a seesaw and if they went on it with another child who was about the same size or someone who was larger or smaller. Review what it means to balance in reference to a seesaw. You might want to introduce the concept of simple machines and the main types: levers, wedges, inclined planes, pulleys, and wheels.

Center Preparation

Materials: 1 wooden ruler, 12" (30 cm) in length; 2 flat fishing sinkers, 1-2 ounces (28-57 g) each; 2 lighter flat fishing sinkers, 0.5 ounce (14 g) each; 1 hexagonal pencil

Directions: The lever needed for this experiment is best made from a thick wooden ruler. Thin wooden rulers or plastic ones will bend when the weights are put at each end and the seesaw will not work correctly. Be sure to use a hexagonal pencil for the fulcrum. A round pencil will not work well because it can roll.

You will need to have two heavy weights and two light weights that are flat and can be stacked. Flat fishing sinkers work well for this and are available in discount department stores and sports supply stores. They come in sizes that reflect their weight in ounces (grams). The heavier sinkers should weigh at least twice as much as the lighter ones. As an alternative to sinkers, hexagonal nuts, available in hardware stores, also work. However, you will have to find two sizes of the appropriate weights.

Follow-Up Activities

Allow students to try different combinations of weights and fulcrum positions to better understand levers.

Talk about how levers are used in balance scales. If possible demonstrate how to use a balance scale. Point out the fulcrum. Review the meaning of the word *balance*.

Name: _____ Date: _____

Seesaw Science

Lab Worksheet — Level A

Ask Yourself

Can a big child and a small child ride a seesaw together?

What You Need

_____ 1 ruler

_____ 1 pencil

_____ 2 big weights

_____ 2 small weights

What You Do

_____ 1. Put the pencil under the middle of the ruler.

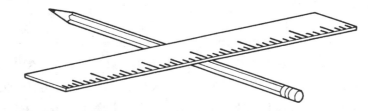

_____ 2. Put a big weight on each end of the ruler.

_____ 3. Does the seesaw work well? _____Yes   _____No

_____ 4. Now try a small weight on one end and a big weight on the other end.

_____ 5. Does the seesaw work well? _____Yes   _____No

_____ 6. How can you make the seesaw work with these weights? _____

_____

What You Learned

How did you make the seesaw work with the small weight on one end and a big weight on the other end? Use the space below to draw a picture of what you did.

Name: _____ Date: _____

Seesaw Science

Lab Worksheet — Level B

Ask Yourself

Can children of different sizes ride a seesaw together? _____

What You Need

_____ 1 ruler   _____ 2 heavy weights
_____ 1 pencil   _____ 2 light weights

What You Do

_____ 1. Build a seesaw by putting the pencil under the middle of the ruler.

_____ 2. Pretend the two heavy weights are two large children who want to seesaw. Put one heavy weight on each end of the ruler, and see if the seesaw will work. Does the seesaw work? _____ Can you make it balance? _____

_____

_____ 3. Now pretend that a light weight is a large child's little brother who wants a turn on the seesaw. Replace one of the heavy weights with one of the light weights. What happens to the seesaw? Can you make it balance? _____

_____ 4. Try putting two light weights on one end and one heavy weight on the other end. Does the seesaw work? _____ Can you make it balance?

_____

_____ 5. Pretend that there are not any other small children who can sit with the little brother. Can you find a way to change the seesaw so that the little brother, by himself, can ride opposite a large child? Find a way to make your seesaw work easily with a large weight on one side and a small weight on the other.

What You Learned

How did you change the seesaw so that it would balance with a heavy weight on one side and a light weight on the other side? To show what you did, draw a diagram with labels on the back of this paper. Under your diagram, write a description of the changes you made.

Wedges

Background

A wedge is a simple machine that changes the direction of a force. If you put the tip of a wedge between two objects and push down, the objects will move apart. Thus a vertical force is translated into a horizontal one. There are more wedges around us than most of us realize. Nails are wedges that can be used to split a piece of wood. Knives are also wedges. For example, you can push down on a simple butter knife to separate a slice of butter from the stick. Other wedges include forks, doorstops, and zippers.

Objectives

- To become familiar with the basic function of a wedge.
- To make specific observations that can be used to deduce a general rule about how wedges work.

Student Instruction

Review how to measure, using a ruler. Have students recall the types of simple machines: wedges, inclined planes, wheels, pulleys, and levers. Explain that a wedge is a type of inclined plane. Give some examples of inclined planes: a ramp, a wedge type doorstop, a playground slide. Ask volunteers to provide other examples.

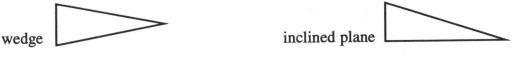

wedge   inclined plane

Center Preparation

Materials: 1 thin wedge; 1 fat wedge; 2 blocks; 1 ruler, 12" (30 cm) in length

Directions: Buy or make two wedges of different thickness. You can buy small, long, 1" (2.5 cm) plastic wedges in hardware stores. Make a large wedge by cutting a 2' x 4' (0.6 m x 1.2 m) piece of wood at approximately 60 degree angles. As an alternative, you could cut 3-4 pieces of corrugated cardboard and glue them together to form a wedge.

The two blocks must be the same size, but they can be from many sources. They can be counting blocks used in math, 3" (7.5 cm) long blocks cut from the 2' x 4' (0.6 m x 1.2 m) piece of wood, building blocks, or even small cardboard boxes. Whatever material you choose for the blocks, it should be lightweight.

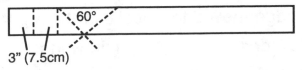

Follow-Up Activities

Encourage students to take another look around for wedges and inclined planes. This time students will have a better understanding of these simple machines so they may spot nails, scissors, knives, zippers, and other less obvious examples.

Name: _____ Date: _____

Wedges

Lab Worksheet — Level A

Ask Yourself

What does a wedge do?

What You Need

____ 2 blocks

____ 1 fat wedge

____ 1 thin wedge

What You Do

____ 1. Put the two blocks side by side.

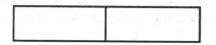

____ 2. Put the fat wedge where the two blocks meet.

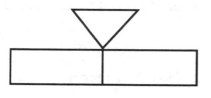

____ 3. Push down on the wedge.

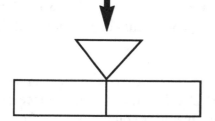

____ 4. Now repeat Steps 1, 2, and 3 with the thin wedge.

____ 5. Which wedge moved the blocks farther apart?

____ fat wedge   ____ thin wedge

What You Learned

When you pushed down on the wedge, what happened to the blocks? _____

_____

Name: _____ Date: _____

Wedges

Lab Worksheet — Level B

Ask Yourself

What does a wedge do? _____

_____

What You Need

_____ 2 blocks   _____ 1 thin wedge

_____ 1 fat wedge   _____ 1 ruler

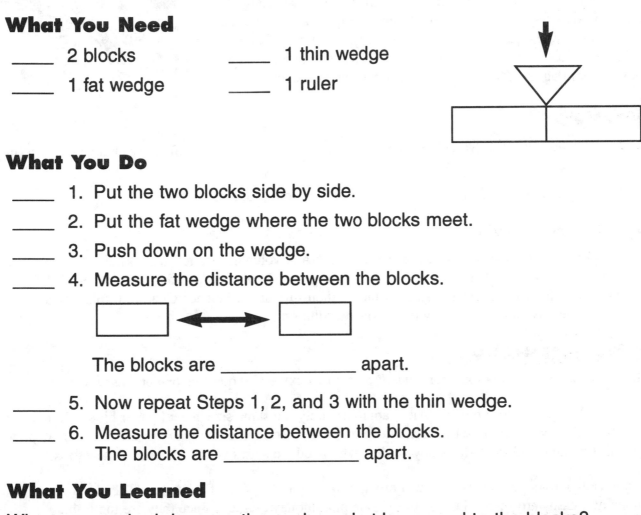

What You Do

_____ 1. Put the two blocks side by side.

_____ 2. Put the fat wedge where the two blocks meet.

_____ 3. Push down on the wedge.

_____ 4. Measure the distance between the blocks.

The blocks are _____ apart.

_____ 5. Now repeat Steps 1, 2, and 3 with the thin wedge.

_____ 6. Measure the distance between the blocks.
The blocks are _____ apart.

What You Learned

When you pushed down on the wedge, what happened to the blocks? _____

_____

Which wedge moved the blocks farther apart? _____

How much farther did the blocks move? _____

$1.25

Background

Creating modern structures, such as skyscrapers and other buildings, takes materials that are lightweight but strong. Strength can be obtained by making a material thicker. However, in the case of a wood beam, it gets heavier as you increase the thickness. Some materials can be made stronger by changing their shapes rather than increasing the amount of materials used. A steel I-beam is an example of this. By making the cross sections form the letter I, the beam is as strong as a solid beam that weighs and costs much more. Paper can also be much stronger than we realize if we shape it correctly. Folding a dollar bill in half and then standing it on its edge makes it strong enough to support a quarter. Folding the dollar bill several times makes it even stronger.

Objectives

- To introduce the idea that the strength of some materials can be significantly changed by altering their shapes.

- To use trial and error as a means to find a solution to a problem.

Student Instruction

Talk about bridges, skyscrapers, and other structures. Ask volunteers to tell what kinds of materials are used to make these. The idea for making paper stronger is simple. Ask students not to tell their classmates how the experiment works after taking their turn at the Science Center. Explain that everyone should have an opportunity to discover a solution.

Center Preparation

Materials: play dollar bills, one per student plus a few extras; 10 quarters or flat washers; 1 ruler

Directions: Use play paper money that is approximately the same size as real paper bills. Do not use real dollar bills since they may be worn out from having been folded so many times. Use a new play dollar bill for each student. Allow any student who needs to start over to use one of the extras.

You can use quarters or flat washers that are approximately the size of a quarter. These may be obtained at a hardware store. Do not use plastic play money quarters since they are too light.

Follow-Up Activities

Use four play dollar bills folded as in the experiment and try to hold up as many quarters as you can. You need the four bills so that one can be placed in each corner for balance.

There are limits as to how large a structure can be. Demonstrate this by repeating the experiment with successively taller pieces of paper. Fold each one as students folded their play dollar bills. After the pieces of paper reach a certain height, they become unstable and will no longer support as much weight as the shorter versions.

30

Name: _____ Date: _____

$1.25

Lab Worksheet — Level A

Ask Yourself

Can I use a play dollar bill to hold a quarter off the table?

What You Need

_____ 1 play dollar bill

_____ 10 quarters

What You Do

_____ 1. Find a way to hold one quarter off the table by placing it on the edge of the dollar bill.

_____ 2. What did you do to the dollar bill to make the quarter stay on top?

_____

_____ 3. Add more quarters, one at a time, to the top of the dollar bill.

_____ 4. See if you can make the dollar bill hold up all 10 quarters.

What You Learned

How many quarters did your dollar bill hold up? _____

Draw a picture to show how you did it.

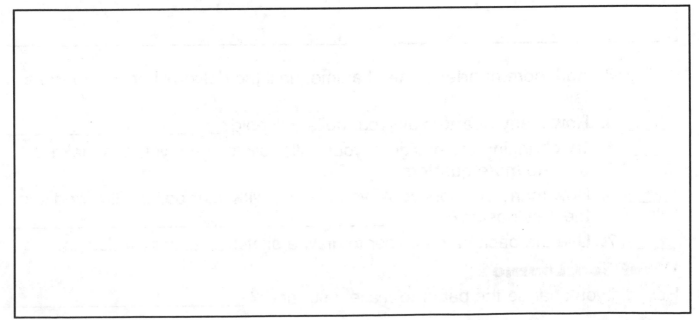

Name: _____   Date: _____

$1.25

Lab Worksheet — Level B

Ask Yourself

How many quarters do I think I can balance on the edge of a piece of paper?

_____

What You Need

_____   1 play dollar bill

_____   1 ruler

_____   10 quarters

What You Do

_____   1. Experiment until you can find a way to hold one quarter about
2 inches (5 cm) off the table using only the play dollar bill.

_____   2. Draw a sketch to show what you did.

First Design	Final Design

_____   3. Add more quarters, one at a time, until the dollar bill or the quarters
fall.

_____   4. How many quarters did your dollar bill hold?_____

_____   5. Try changing the design of your dollar bill to see if you can make it
hold up more quarters.

_____   6. How many quarters could you hold up with your dollar bill folded into
the new design?_____

_____   7. Use the back of this paper to draw a sketch of your new design.

What You Learned

How did you change the paper to make it stronger? _____

Ball and Boat

Background

A ball of clay sinks if we drop it in water. However, if we shape it into a flat, wide boat, it will float. The scientific principle involved here is the one that caused Archimedes (287-212 B.C.), a Greek mathematician, engineer, and physicist, to shout out "Eureka!" while taking a bath. The amount of water an object displaces is equal to the volume of the object. If the weight of that displaced water is greater than the weight of the object, the object will float. By shaping the clay into a boat, we increase its effective volume without changing its weight. Therefore, we increase its buoyancy.

Objectives

- To realize that the shape of materials affects their buoyancy.
- To make and then test predictions.

Student Instruction

On the chalkboard, draw a two-column chart with the headings *Sink* and *Float*. Have students brainstorm two lists: objects that sink in water and objects that float. Write their responses on the chart under the appropriate heading. Then ask students if they can think of any objects that sink part way. You may wish to add a third column to your chart for these responses.

Point out to students that the water in a bathtub rises when they get into it. Ask them to recall if the water rises more when they are standing up or lying down in the tub. They may have noticed that the more of the body (greater volume) that goes into the water, the more water is displaced, and the higher it rises.

Center Preparation

Materials: 8 sticks of clay, 2 quart (1.9 mL) mixing bowl or a shallow bucket, water, bath towel, paper towels

Directions: Cover the work area with a bath towel to soak up the inevitable drips and spills. Pour approximately 2 inches (5 cm) of water into the bowl or shallow bucket. Each student will need enough modeling clay to make a ball that is approximately 1-2 inches (2.5-5 cm) in diameter. If you buy the clay in sticks, you will need one stick for every three students. The clay gets soft when it is repeatedly mixed and kneaded with water, so it becomes impractical to reuse it many times. **Helpful Hint:** Drying the clay on a paper towel before reshaping it will help remove the water and make it easier to reshape.

Follow-Up Activities

Test students' boat designs to see which one holds the most weight. Use large hexagonal nuts or any other identical, small but heavy objects. You should find that the flattest, widest boat holds the most weight, assuming it is stable enough to stay upright without tipping over.

Name: _____ Date: _____

Ball and Boat

Lab Worksheet — Level A

Ask Yourself

Can I make clay float?

What You Need

_____ 1 piece of clay

_____ 1 bowl or bucket of water

_____ 1 paper towel

What You Do

_____ 1. Make a ball out of the clay.

_____ 2. Predict: Do you think that it will sink or float? _____

_____ 3. Put the clay ball in the water. Did it sink or float? _____

_____ 4. Dry the clay ball with the paper towel.

_____ 5. Now shape the clay to look like a boat.

_____ 6. Predict: Do you think that the clay boat will sink or float? _____

_____ 7. Put the clay boat in the water. Did it sink or float? _____

_____ 8. If your clay boat did not float, try to make a different boat shape that will float.

What You Learned

Can you make clay float? _____ Yes   _____ No

Draw a picture of your clay boat that floated.

Name: _____ Date: _____

Ball and Boat

Lab Worksheet — Level B

Ask Yourself

Can I make clay float? _____

What You Need

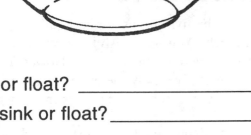

____ 1 piece of clay

____ 1 bowl or bucket of water

____ 1 paper towel

What You Do

____ 1. Make a ball out of the clay.

____ 2. Predict: Do you think that it will sink or float? _____

____ 3. Put the clay ball in the water. Did it sink or float? _____

____ 4. Dry the clay ball with the paper towel.

____ 5. Change the shape of the clay until you can make it float.

____ 6. Dry the clay with the paper towel, and make it into a ball again.

____ 7. Predict: Do you think that it will sink or float? _____

____ 8. Put the clay ball in the water. What happened? _____

What You Learned

Could you make the clay float?_____

Describe the shape that was needed for the clay to float. _____

_____

_____

_____

Blind Balance

Background

We use our senses in more ways than we realize. For instance, did you know that you use your eyes to balance? Try standing on one foot. Now experiment to see if it is easier to balance when you are looking down, up at the ceiling, to the side, or straight ahead. Most of us find it easiest to balance when looking at a non-moving object across the room. For an even more dramatic example of how vision affects balance, stand on one foot and then close your eyes. Most people immediately lose their balance.

Objectives

- To make students more aware of the senses, how we use them, and how they are interconnected.
- To introduce the concept of experimental error and the need to take multiple measurements.

Student Instruction

Review the five senses: sight, hearing, smell, taste, and touch. You may wish to allow students to practice standing on one foot. However, be sure you do not give away the experiment. Show your class how to record their results in the table.

Teach students how to use a stopwatch or the second hand on a clock. For students who will be working at Level A, talk about and practice counting at a consistent, steady rate.

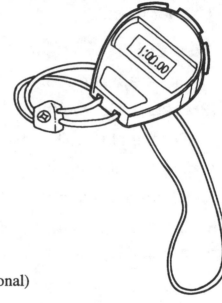

Center Preparation

Materials: 1 stopwatch or clock with a second hand (optional)

Directions: You may wish to have students use a stopwatch or a clock with a second hand. Make sure you allow enough space for students to stand on one foot and stumble a little bit without getting hurt.

Follow-Up Activities

See if students can think of ways in which the senses are interconnected. Example questions: *Can you taste food when you have a stuffy nose? Is it easier to hear or distinguish sounds when your eyes are open or closed?*

For the Level B activity, review students' results for the differences in balancing times between the left and right feet.

Talk about the differences in the three successive measurements and what sort of variables or experimental error might account for them. Discuss why it is important to take multiple measurements and not just assume that the first measurement is conclusive.

Name: _____ Date: _____

Blind Balance

Lab Worksheet — Level A

Ask Yourself

Do I use my eyes to balance?

What You Need

_____ Your body

What You Do

_____ 1. Stand on one foot with your **eyes open** as long as you can.

_____ 2. Count slowly to see how long you can balance.

_____ 3. Write the count in the table shown below.

_____ 4. Do this two more times.

_____ 5. Stand on one foot with your **eyes closed** as long as you can.

_____ 6. Count slowly to see how long you can balance.

_____ 7. Write the count in the table shown below.

_____ 8. Do this two more times.

	How Long Can You Stand on One Foot?		
	1	2	3
Eyes Open			
Eyes Closed			

What You Learned

Do you use your eyes to balance?

_____ Yes   _____ No

Name: _____ Date: _____

Blind Balance

Lab Worksheet — Level B

Ask Yourself

Do I use my eyes to balance? _____

What You Need

_____ 1 stopwatch   _____ Your body

What You Do

_____ 1. Stand on your right foot with your eyes open as long as you can.
_____ 2. Use the stopwatch to time how long you can balance.
_____ 3. Write the time in the table shown below.
_____ 4. Do this two more times.
_____ 5. Now stand on your left foot with your eyes open as long as you can.
_____ 6. Use the stopwatch to time how long you can balance.
_____ 7. Write the time in the table.
_____ 8. Do this two more times.
_____ 9. Which foot is easier to balance on?_____
_____ 10. With your eyes closed, stand on the foot that it was easier for you to balance on.
_____ 11. Time yourself and write the time in the table.
_____ 12. Do this two more times.

	How Long Can You Stand on One Foot?		
	1	2	3
Right Foot, Eyes Open			
Left Foot, Eyes Open			
_____ Foot, Eyes Closed			

What You Learned

What happens when you close your eyes while balancing on one foot? Do you use your eyes to balance? Write your answers on the back of this paper.

Mystery Cans

Background

Can we tell what an object is without seeing it? We can because we use other senses to collect indirect evidence. With this information it is relatively easy to determine the identity of the object or, at least, some of its characteristics.

Objectives

- To learn that the senses collect redundant information so that you are not completely dependent on any one of them.

- To gather and use indirect evidence to identify an object or its characteristics.

Student Instruction

Review the five senses and the normal uses of each. If students have already done the experiment Blind Balance (pages 36-38), review how the senses are interrelated. Give examples of how people who are unable to use one of their senses can still function. Talk about the experiment and how students might go about finding out what is in each mystery can. Tell the class not to open the cans.

Introduce the concept of indirect evidence. Explain that scientists often have to infer the existence or characteristics of something they cannot actually see.

Center Preparation

Materials: 6-10 empty, opaque 35 mm film cans; small objects

Directions: You should prepare 6-10 mystery cans. If you do not have any film cans, ask stores that develop film if they have any that they can give you. Use a permanent marker to label the lid of each can with a letter of the alphabet. Make sure that each can has a different letter.

Select some common objects from around your classroom or home that will fit in the mystery cans. Suggested items include pencil erasers, paper clips, buttons, marbles, small pieces of chalk, small pieces of paper, push pins, toothpicks, pennies. Put two of an object in each can and snap on the lids. To better secure the lids on the cans, use tape.

For students using Lab Worksheet — Level A (page 40), list the items in random order on the lines for Step 2. For students using Level B (page 41), use an index card to write a list of the items you used, and place it in the center. Do not indicate which item is in each can. You may wish to add a few extra items to the list to make the exercise more challenging. Keep a list of what is in each can for your own reference.

Follow-Up Activities

Have students wear blindfolds, and try to move around the classroom. Discuss what clues and signals they use to know where they are or where to move. To avoid accidents, have only a couple of students wear the blindfolds at one time, and caution them to move slowly.

Name: _____ Date: _____

Mystery Cans

Lab Worksheet — Level A

Ask Yourself

Can I tell what an object is if I cannot see it?

What You Need

_____ 6 mystery cans

What You Do

_____ 1. Try to find out what is in each can without opening it.

_____ 2. Draw a line to match the letter of each can to the name of the object you think is inside.

Can	Object
A	_____
B	_____
C	_____
D	_____
E	_____
F	_____

What You Learned

How could you tell what was in each can?_____

_____

Which senses did you use?

_____ sight   _____ smell

_____ touch   _____ taste

_____ hearing

Name: _____   Date: _____

Mystery Cans

Lab Worksheet — Level B

Ask Yourself

How can I tell what an object is if I cannot see it? _____

What You Need

____   1 set of mystery cans

____   List of mystery items

What You Do

____   1. Try to figure out what is in each can without opening it.

____   2. Use the chart shown below to write down your observations about each can.

____   3. Now write what you think is in each can.

Can	Observation	Object
A		
B		
C		
D		
E		
F		
G		
H		
I		
J		

What You Learned

What senses did you use to figure out what the objects were even though you could not see them? _____

_____

_____

Classifying Leaves

Background

Leaves are often little green things with pointy edges. Does this mean that all leaves are alike? No, there are thousands of different kinds of leaves. If we look closely at each leaf, we will see an enormous amount of detail such as the pattern of its veins, the stomata on the back of it, its thickness, its shape, and its texture. This experiment gives students a chance to explore leaves in detail. Since leaves have such a wide variety of characteristics, we can use them to model how scientists classify things.

Objectives

- To become aware of variety in nature and understand the basic principles of classification.

- To increase students' powers of observation to include details that may otherwise be overlooked.

Student Instruction

Talk about different kinds of leaves. Show pictures of leaves and see how many students can name. Talk about the function of leaves and the changes they undergo during the year. Select two obviously different leaves such as a maple leaf and an oak leaf. Show the real leaves or pictures of them. Discuss with your class how these leaves are alike and how they are different. Ask students to suggest reasons that scientists classify living things. Review the basics of that classification system.

If students will be bringing leaves to class, discuss ecologically sound methods of collecting samples. Remind them that the best way to gather samples is to pick up leaves that have fallen to the ground. If they are taking a sample from a live plant, they should have an adult help them cut off only one leaf so as not to damage the plant. You may also wish to discuss safety issues and show pictures of plants, such as poison ivy, that should be avoided.

Make sure students know how to use a magnifying glass.

Center Preparation

Materials: 1 magnifying glass, 12 leaves

Directions: Have each student bring to class twelve leaves from different kinds of plants, including trees. If you prefer, you can provide the leaves students will use. If students collect the leaves, they will have fun examining their own samples. On the other hand, if everyone uses the same samples, it will be easier to compare results and observations.

Follow-Up Activities

If students brought their own leaves to class, have them sort the leaves according to like characteristics. Then ask them to make posters showing the different groups. Help them label the different groups of leaves according to the like characteristics.

Provide pictures of flowers or animals. Allow students to sort the pictures according to like characteristics. Discuss the different groups that they create.

Name: _____ Date: _____

Classifying Leaves
Lab Worksheet — Level A

Ask Yourself

How can I classify leaves?

What You Need

_____ 12 different leaves

What You Do

_____ 1. Look closely at all of your leaves.

_____ 2. Find a characteristic that some of the leaves have in common. Put those leaves in a separate pile. Use a box at the bottom of page 44 to show the leaves in this group.

_____ 3. Write the common characteristic here: Some of the leaves have
_____.

_____ 4. How many leaves have this characteristic?_____

How many leaves do not have this characteristic?_____

_____ 5. Put all of the leaves back in one pile.

_____ 6. Look at the leaves and find a different characteristic that some of them have in common. Put those leaves in a separate pile. Use a box at the bottom of page 44 to show the leaves in this group.

_____ 7. Write the common characteristic here: Some of the leaves have
_____.

_____ 8. How many leaves have this characteristic?_____

How many leaves do not have this characteristic?_____

Name: _____ Date: _____

Classifying Leaves (cont.)

Lab Worksheet — Level A (cont.)

_____ 9. Put all of the leaves back in one pile.

_____ 10. Look at the leaves, and find a different characteristic that some of them have in common. Put those leaves in a separate pile. Use a box at the bottom the page to show the leaves in this group.

_____ 11. Write the common characteristic here: Some of the leaves have

_____.

_____ 12. How many leaves have this characteristic?_____

How many leaves do not have this characteristic?_____

What You Learned

What characteristics can be used to classify leaves? _____
_____

Is there only one way to classify leaves?
_____ Yes _____ No

Draw pictures to show the three groups of leaves that you made.

Name: _____ Date: _____

Classifying Leaves

Lab Worksheet — Level B

Ask Yourself

What characteristics can I use to classify leaves? _____

_____

What You Need

____ 12 different leaves   ____ 1 magnifying glass

What You Do

____ 1. Look closely at your leaves. You can use the magnifying glass.

____ 2. Find a characteristic that some of the leaves have in common.

____ 3. Write the characteristic in the table shown below Step 7.

____ 4. Divide the leaves into two piles: those that have this characteristic and those that do not.

____ 5. Count the number of leaves in each pile, and write the information in the table under the correct heading.

____ 6. Put all of the leaves back in one pile. Find a different characteristic that some of the leaves have in common. Repeat Steps 3, 4, and 5 for this characteristic.

____ 7. Put all of the leaves back in one pile. Repeat Steps 2-5 until you have at least five characteristics that can be used to separate the leaves into different groups.

	Characteristic	Number of leaves with characteristic	Number of leaves without characteristic
1.			
2.			
3.			
4.			
5.			

What You Learned

What are some different ways that you can classify leaves?

Insect or Not?

Background

Most students think that all bugs are insects. This experiment will help them realize that this is not true. They will start to appreciate the details that help to differentiate bugs and insects.

Objectives

- To learn the difference between bugs and insects.
- To improve students' powers of observation and review the idea of classification.

Student Instruction

Review the animal kingdoms, the general idea of classification, and how to put data in a table. Talk about the characteristics of insects: six legs, exoskeleton, and three body segments. Also discuss the characteristics of other closely related animals such as spiders, ticks, and centipedes. Talk about the differences between what we commonly refer to as bugs (any wingless or four-winged insect; mouthparts used for piercing and sucking) and insects (usually small invertebrates with an exoskeleton; adults have six legs, three body segments, and two pairs of wings).

Center Preparation

Materials: 8-12 plastic bugs

Directions: You will need to collect 8-12 small plastic bugs. Try to get an assortment of spiders, worms, ants, flies, beetles, centipedes, butterflies, and, if possible, a scorpion. These can often be purchased where novelties or party favors are sold or in the trinket machines found in grocery stores. Some students may own the toy that makes bugs by cooking liquid plastic and would be willing to make some for the class.

Label each specimen with a letter of the alphabet. To do the labeling, you can use a permanent marker and masking tape, or you can glue each plastic bug to an index card and label the card. Make sure all the legs are visible.

Follow-Up Activities

Talk about how to classify animals. Ask students what types of characteristics they could use to classify animals.

Let students develop their own classification systems by separating the set of bugs into groups that share common characteristics.

Name: _____ Date: _____

Insect or Not?

Lab Worksheet — Level A

Ask Yourself

Are all bugs insects?

What You Need

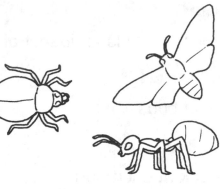

_____ 1 set of bugs

What You Do

_____ 1. Count the legs on each bug.

_____ 2. Write the number of legs on each bug in the table under Step 3.

_____ 3. Put an **X** under *Yes* if you think the bug is an insect. Put an **X** under *No* if you do not think the bug is an insect.

Bug	Number of Legs	Is this an insect?	
		Yes	No
A			
B			
C			
D			
E			
F			
G			
H			

What You Learned

Are all bugs insects? _____ Yes _____ No

Name: _____ Date: _____

Insect or Not?

Lab Worksheet — Level B

Ask Yourself

How can I tell if a bug is an insect or not?

What You Need

_____ 1 set of bugs

What You Do

_____ 1. Look at each bug.

_____ 2. Fill out the table shown below to tell about each bug.

Bug	Is this an insect?		Why or why not?
	Yes	No	
A			
B			
C			
D			
E			
F			
G			
H			
I			
J			

What You Learned

How can you tell if a bug is an insect or not?_____

_____

Magical Magnets

Background

There are three types of metals that are magnetic: iron, nickel, and cobalt. If an item contains one of these metals, a magnet will stick to it. Otherwise, it will not.

Objectives

- To acquaint students with magnets and the idea that some materials are magnetic and some are not.

- To deduce a general rule about magnetism from specific observations.

Student Instruction

Talk about what objects in your classroom are made of: wood, plastic, paper, metal. Explain that many objects are made from more than one type of material. Point out to students that there are different types of metals. Tell them that some metal objects are actually made from a combination of metals. Talk about the things they can observe when examining a metal: color, softness, density, etc.

Center Preparation

Materials: 1 magnet; 10-12 small objects such as a paper clip, penny, dime, brad (paper fastener), safety pin, metal scissors, chalk, paper, crayon, pen, pencil, book, eraser, rubber band

Directions: Provide a magnet. A magnet that is round, about ½ inch (1.25 cm) in diameter, and is used for hanging things on walls is ideal because it should be fairly strong. **Helpful Hint:** When the magnet gets dropped and cannot be found, remember to check the metal legs of the desk or the underside of metal shelves. Collect a sample of 10-12 readily recognizable objects from around the classroom. Make sure to include several that are made of metal and several that are not. For younger students, write the names of the objects on Lab Worksheet — Level A (page 50) before reproducing it.

Follow-Up Activities

Review where students think magnets will stick in the classroom and why. Then allow them to test their theories.

Use magnets to test food and beverage cans of different types. See if your students can determine that aluminum beverage cans are not magnetic while steel or bimetal cans are. Explain that this property is used in the recycling process to separate the different types of metal before processing.

Allow students to test the strength of the magnet by seeing how many of one type of object, such as paper clips, it can pick up.

Provide different types of magnets for students to examine and use. Have them discuss how the magnets are alike and different.

Show students how to magnetize a needle by rubbing it in one direction on a bar magnet. Allow them to carefully experiment with the magnetized needle.

Name: _____ Date: _____

Magical Magnets

Lab Worksheet — Level A

Ask Yourself

Will all things stick to magnets?

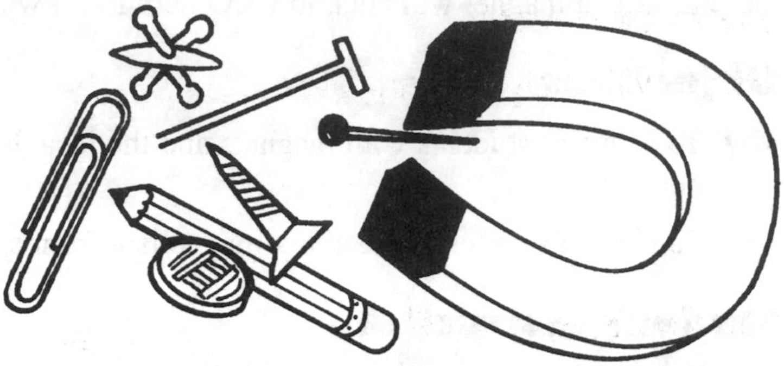

What You Need

____ 1 magnet

____ Set of items to test

What You Do

____ 1. Touch each item with the magnet. See which ones will stick to the magnet.

____ 2. Use the chart below to write whether or not each item sticks to the magnet.

Item	Sticks to Magnet?	
	Yes	No
1.		
2.		
3.		
4.		
5.		
6.		
7.		
8.		
9.		
10.		

What You Learned

Will all things stick to magnets? _____ Yes _____ No

Name: _____ Date: _____

Magical Magnets

Lab Worksheet — Level B

Ask Yourself

What will stick to magnets? _____

_____

_____

What You Need

____ 1 magnet

____ Set of items to test

What You Do

____ 1. In the chart on page 52, write the name of each item that you will test.

____ 2. Write in the chart what you think each item is made of.

____ 3. Touch each item with the magnet. See which ones stick to it.

____ 4. Record your observations in the chart.

____ 5. Pick two more items from your classroom to test. Repeat Steps 1-4 for these items.

What You Learned

Name the items that stuck to the magnet.

_____

_____

What do these items have in common?

_____

_____

Will all items made from metal stick to magnets?

_____

Name: _____ Date: _____

Magical Magnets (cont.)

Lab Worksheet — Level B (cont.)

Use the chart shown below to record your lab results from page 51.

Item	What is it made of?	Does it stick to the magnet?	
		Yes	No
1.			
2.			
3.			
4.			
5.			
6.			
7.			
8.			
9.			
10.			
11.			
12.			

Static Electricity

Background

Rubbing a balloon with a piece of wool gives the balloon an electrical charge. This electrical charge makes it stick to the uncharged wall. To discharge the balloon, wipe it with your hands or a damp paper towel. This is the same effect you see when, on a cold, dry winter day you pull a sweater over your head and your hair stands on end. Dampening your hair causes it to settle back down. If you charge two balloons, the similar electrical charges repel each other and the balloons will push apart.

We can also easily charge other plastic items, such as drinking straws, and use the attractive force of the static electricity to pick up light weight objects such as pepper. Heavier objects, such as salt crystals, are less likely to be lifted.

Objective

- To introduce the concept of static electricity and electrical charge.

Student Instruction

Do some demonstrations to introduce static electricity. Use the following suggestions, or create some of your own. Rub a balloon on your head and then stick the balloon to a wall. Rub a balloon on a wool sweater and then hold it over the head of a student who has fine, straight hair that is a few inches long. This should make the hair stand on end. Tie two balloons to two strings, each one foot (0.3 m) long. Tie the other end of the strings together and hang up the balloons so that they are touching. Now rub each balloon with a piece of wool felt or a wool sweater. Students should note that the balloons repel each other. Talk about how you are charging these balloons with electricity, causing them to be attracted to objects that have not been charged and repelled by objects that have been charged. For students using Lab Worksheet — Level B (page 55), review the meaning of *horizontal* and *vertical*.

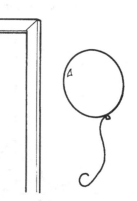

Center Preparation

Materials: plastic straws, one per student; salt shaker with salt in it; pepper shaker with pepper in it; white scrap papers; paper towels or rags

Directions: This center requires one plastic straw for each student. Although a straw could be used many times, for health reasons it is best to give each student a new one. Each student will also need a few shakes each from a salt and pepper shaker. A piece of white scrap paper for each student to work on makes clean up easier. Students will need damp (not wet) paper towels or a rag to make sure the straw is discharged at the beginning of the experiment.

Follow-Up Activities

Ask students to see what other objects, such as scraps of paper or chalk dust, the straw will pick up.

Allow them to try rubbing the straw with different materials to see if it picks up objects better.

Name: _____ Date: _____

Static Electricity
Lab Worksheet — Level A

Ask Yourself

Can I pick up salt and pepper without touching it?

What You Need

_____ 1 straw

_____ 1 piece of white paper

_____ 1 salt shaker

_____ 1 pepper shaker

_____ 1 damp paper towel or rag

What You Do

_____ 1. Shake the salt shaker one time over the white paper. Do the same with the pepper so that it mixes with the salt.

_____ 2. Wipe the straw with the damp paper towel or rag.

_____ 3. Hold the straw like a wand, and move it over the salt and pepper.

_____ 4. Does anything change?   _____ Yes   _____ No

_____ 5. Rub the straw across your hair ten times.

_____ 6. Hold the straw like a wand, and move it over the salt and pepper.

If nothing happens, do Steps 5 and 6 again.

What You Learned

What happened?

_____ Mostly the salt jumped up.

_____ Mostly the pepper jumped up.

Name: _____ Date: _____

Static Electricity

Lab Worksheet — Level B

Ask Yourself

If salt and pepper are mixed together, how can I separate them? _____

_____

What You Need

- _____ 1 straw
- _____ 1 piece of white paper
- _____ 1 salt shaker
- _____ 1 pepper shaker
- _____ 1 damp paper towel or rag

What You Do

- _____ 1. Shake the salt shaker one time over the white paper. Do the same with the pepper so that it mixes with the salt.
- _____ 2. Wipe the straw with the damp paper towel or rag.
- _____ 3. Hold the straw horizontally and move it over the salt and pepper.
- _____ 4. What happens? _____

  _____

- _____ 5. Now rub the straw across your hair ten times.
- _____ 6. Once again, hold the straw horizontally and move it over the salt and pepper.
- _____ 7. What happens? _____

  _____

What You Learned

How can you use static electricity to separate salt and pepper that are mixed together?

_____

_____

See the Light

Background

A light bulb lights when electrical current flows through the filament, a special type of wire in the bulb. Electrical current will only flow in a closed circuit, or loop of wire. So, to make the light bulb light, you need to connect one wire to the top of the battery and one wire to the bottom. Electrons can then flow out of the battery, through the wire to the light bulb and back through the other wire into the battery.

Objectives

* To increase students' familiarity with electricity.
* To learn how to document observations with a sketch or diagram.

Student Instruction

Review how we use electricity and the important role it plays in our society.

The voltage of a battery is only 1.5 volts compared to the 110 or 220 volts used in household electricity. Emphasize that, while this experiment is completely safe, the power delivered from electrical outlets is dangerous and should never be experimented with.

Explain that students may want to tape some of the components together so they do not have to hold all of them. However, they should remove all of the tape when they are finished.

Center Preparation

Materials: 2 flashlight bulbs; 2 wires, each 4-6" (10-15 cm) long; 1 D-cell (flashlight) battery; masking tape

Directions: The instructions for making all of the electrical components are on page 57. You can buy flashlight bulbs and special holders from many school science equipment suppliers. However, it is less expensive and easier to use old Christmas tree lights. You only need one D-cell (flashlight battery) to light a bulb. The two wires can be obtained by cutting pieces from the old string of Christmas tree lights. These wires are not necessary if you use Christmas tree lights, but they provide some other options for students to explore.

Follow-Up Activities

Help the class relate the experiment to their homes. The light bulb is easily identified as a lamp. We get our household electricity from a power plant, not a battery. The wires that connect the lamp to the outlet are also visible as the lamp cord. However, the ones that run through the walls and to and from the power plant are not as obvious.

See the Light (cont.)

Construction Instructions

To make a light bulb from Christmas tree lights:

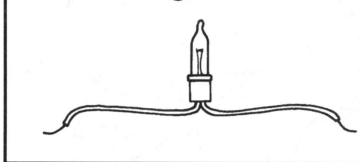

Cut out one light bulb leaving the wires attached. Strip off 0.5-1" (1.25-2.5 cm) of the plastic coating from the end of each wire. To do this, cut through the plastic with scissors, being careful not to cut the wires. Then pull the cut piece of plastic coating off the end of each wire.

To make a wire:

Cut a piece of wire 6-9" (15-23 cm) long from the string of light bulbs. Strip off 0.5-1" (1.25-2.5 cm) of the plastic coating from each end of the wire as described above.

To make a continuity tester:

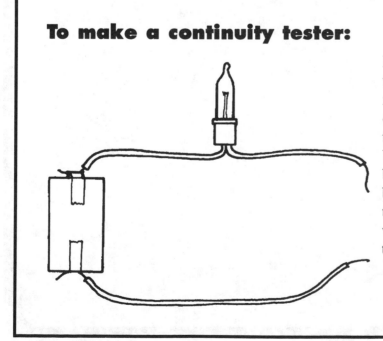

Make a light bulb and a wire following the instructions shown above. Use masking tape to connect the bare end of one wire coming out of the light bulb to the top of a D-cell (flashlight) battery. Use masking tape to connect one of the bare ends of the wire (without a light bulb) to the bottom of the battery. Close the circuit by touching the remaining two wire ends. If your tester is built properly, the bulb will light.

Name: _____ Date: _____

See the Light

Lab Worksheet — Level A

Ask Yourself

How do I light a light bulb?

What You Need

_____ 1 flashlight bulb

_____ 1 battery

_____ 2 wires

_____ Masking tape

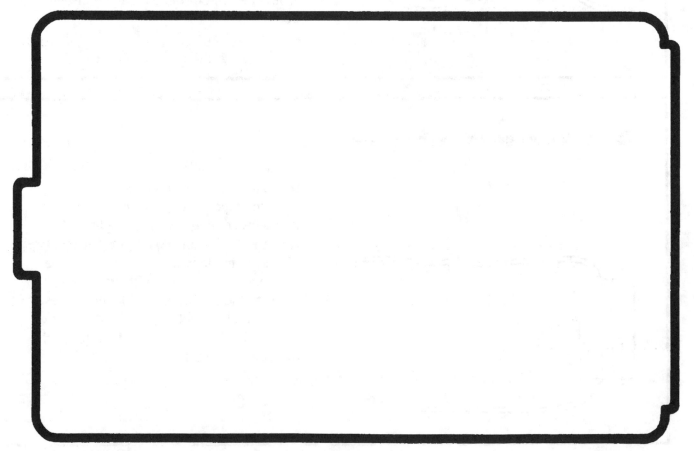

What You Do

_____ Try to get the light bulb to light.

What You Learned

Draw a picture on the battery outline to show how you got the light bulb to light.

Name: _____ Date: _____

See the Light
Lab Worksheet — Level B

Ask Yourself

How does electricity get from a battery to a light bulb? _____

_____

What You Need

____ 2 flashlight bulbs

____ 1 battery

____ 2 wires

____ Masking tape

What You Do

____ 1. Make one light bulb light.

____ 2. On the back of this paper, draw a sketch to show how you got the light bulb to light.

____ 3. Find other ways to light one bulb. On the back of this paper, draw a sketch of each way you found to light the bulb.

____ 4. What part(s) of the battery must the wires, connected to the light bulb, touch to make it light? _____

____ 5. Now tape together the ends of two wires, one from each light bulb. Make sure the metal parts of the wires are touching before you tape them.

____ 6. Make both bulbs light at the same time.

____ 7. On the back of this paper, draw a sketch of how you made both light bulbs light at the same time.

____ 8. How does the brightness of the two bulbs compare to that of just one bulb? _____

What You Learned

How does electricity get from a battery to a light bulb? _____

_____

Go With the Flow

Background

One of the characteristics that makes electricity useful is that it does not travel equally well through all materials. Materials that allow electricity to flow easily are called conductors. Materials that tend to block the flow of electricity are called insulators. In general, metals are conductors while materials like plastic, rubber, and paper are insulators. Some materials, such as the human body, will conduct electricity somewhat. These kinds of materials are said to have high resistance.

Objectives

- To understand the difference between conductors and insulators.

- To realize that there are differences between things that cannot be seen.

Student Instruction

Review the different types of materials (metal, plastic, paper, wood, etc.), and give students some practice with identifying each. Talk about how you can tell what an object is made of. Show your class how to use the continuity tester (page 57) to see if these materials are conductors or insulators.

The voltage of a battery is only 1.5 volts compared to the 110 or 220 volts used in household electricity. Emphasize that, while this experiment is completely safe, the power delivered from electrical outlets is dangerous and should never be experimented with.

Center Preparation

Materials: 1 continuity tester, a variety of small objects

Directions: Build the simple continuity tester as described on page 57. This will allow students to test different materials to see if they conduct electricity. If the lamp lights when they touch the two wire ends to the material, a closed circuit has been made, which means that electricity must be flowing through the object.

Collect a sample of 10-12 readily recognizable objects from around the classroom. Make sure there are some made of metal and others that are not. The selection might include a paper clip, penny, brad (paper fastener), safety pin, metal scissors, chalk, paper, crayon, pen, pencil, book, eraser. For younger students, write the names of the objects on the Lab Worksheet — Level A (page 61) before reproducing it.

Follow-Up Activities

Compare the results obtained by the class. Some objects may give different results for different students. Example: If the scissors have plastic handles, students who attach the wires to the handles will find that the scissors are an insulator. However, students who attach the wires to the blades will find that the scissors are a conductor.

Name: _____ Date: _____

Go With the Flow

Lab Worksheet — Level A

Ask Yourself

Does electricity flow or move through all things?

What You Need

_____ 1 tester

_____ Set of items to test

What You Do

_____ 1. Hold the loose ends of the two wires together. Does the bulb light?

_____ Yes _____ No

_____ 2. Test each item, one at a time, to see if electricity will travel through it. To test an item, hold the loose ends of the two wires on it without letting the wires touch each other. Each time you test an item, put an **X** under *Yes* if the bulb lights. Put an **X** under *No* if the bulb does not light.

Item	Does the bulb light?	
	Yes	No

What You Learned

Does electricity flow, or move, through all things?
_____ Yes _____ No

Name: _____ Date: _____

Go With the Flow

Lab Worksheet — Level B

Ask Yourself

Will electricity flow through all types of material? _____

_____

What You Need

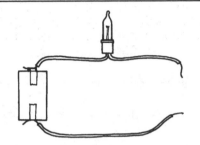

_____ 1 tester

_____ Set of items to test

What You Do

_____ 1. Write the name of each item in the chart on page 63. Record your answers for the following steps on this chart.

_____ 2. Write what you think each item is made of.

_____ 3. Test each item to see if the bulb lights. To test an item, hold the loose ends of the two wires on it without letting the wires touch each other. Put an **X** under *Yes* if the bulb lights. Put an **X** under *No* if the bulb does not light.

_____ 4. Electricity flows through conductors. Electricity does not flow through insulators. Use an **X** to mark whether you think each item is a *conductor* or an *insulator*.

_____ 5. Pick a few more items from around the classroom to test. Repeat Steps 1-4 for these items.

What You Learned

You could tell if electricity flowed through a material being tested because _____

_____

Will electricity flow through all types of materials? Explain your answer. _____

_____

Electrical conductors are made of _____

_____

Name: _____ Date: _____

Go With the Flow (cont.)

Lab Worksheet — Level B (cont.)

Item	What is it made of?	Does the bulb light?		This item is an . . .	
		Yes	No	Conductor	Insulator

Good Vibrations

Background

Sound is caused by vibrations in the air. Any number of things can start air molecules vibrating: a bow being pulled across a violin string, our vocal cords vibrating, or a ruler hitting a metal can. Once a solid object, such as the can, starts vibrating, its molecules push against the neighboring air molecules. The energy from the original vibrations is passed on until it reaches our ear where we hear the sound. These vibrations can also cause a thin membrane (such as a plastic bag pulled tightly over a bowl) to vibrate. Any small objects sitting on the membrane will bounce up and down.

Objective

- To observe the vibrations that are caused by sound.

Student Instruction

Discuss the concept of vibrations with your class. Demonstrate what vibrations are, using a tuning fork, a guitar string, or a rubber band stretched around a milk carton.

Center Preparation

Materials: a 2 quart (1.9 mL) bowl, 1 large rubber band, table salt, 1 thick wooden ruler, 1 small can, 1 piece of plastic

Directions: The bowl should be made of something rigid such as metal or stiff plastic. It should have an opening that is 8-12 inches (20-30 cm) in diameter. The plastic should be fairly strong and a few inches (cm) larger then the opening of the bowl. The side of a plastic grocery bag works well. The rubber band must be large enough to go around the bowl but still fit snugly so that it can hold the plastic tightly. Any small can such as those used for soup, tuna, or pet food will work. Be sure to thoroughly clean the can and remove any sharp edges.

For younger students, you may want to attach the plastic to the bowl in advance. This activity is easier if students work in pairs.

Follow-Up Activities

Another dramatic example of vibrations is to start vibrating a tuning fork, and put its end in a bowl of water. **Helpful Hint:** Be sure to put a towel under the bowl since this can make quite a mess.

This is an excellent opportunity to encourage students to experiment further at home. They could determine the effects of vibrations caused by all sorts of objects: cans of different sizes and shapes, sticks, whistles, etc. To make sure students are learning about science while having fun with this activity, they should make a list of what they are going to test and write what they think will happen before testing the different objects. Afterwards, they should write their results.

Name: _____ Date: _____

Good Vibrations
Lab Worksheet — Level A

Ask Yourself

Can sound make salt move?

What You Need

____ 1 large bowl

____ 1 large rubber band

____ 1 piece of plastic

____ 1 small can

____ 1 ruler

____ Salt

What You Do

____ 1. Put the plastic over the top of the bowl.

____ 2. Use the rubber band to hold the plastic on.

____ 3. Make sure the plastic is tight.

____ 4. Put some salt on the plastic.

____ 5. Hold the small can near the salt.

____ 6. Hit the can with the ruler.

What You Learned

What happened to the salt when you hit the can with the ruler?

_____

_____

_____

_____

Name: _____ Date: _____

Good Vibrations

Lab Worksheet — Level B

Ask Yourself

How can I make salt move without touching it? _____

_____

What You Need

____ 1 large bowl

____ 1 large rubber band

____ 1 piece of plastic

____ 1 small can

____ 1 ruler

____ Salt

What You Do

____ 1. Pull the plastic tightly over the top of the bowl, and hold it in place with the rubber band.

____ 2. Sprinkle some salt on top of the plastic.

____ 3. Hold the small can close to where the salt is, and tap it with the ruler. What happens to the salt?_____

_____

____ 4. Try tapping the small can in different spots and holding it in different directions. Find out how you must hold and tap the can to get the greatest amount of movement from the salt. Describe what works best. _____

_____

What You Learned

What makes the salt bounce up and down? _____

_____

_____

Perfect Pitch

Background

If we talk about making a high sound, are we referring to pitch or volume? (pitch) The concept of pitch is something that many young children do not understand. Even if they understand that there are different musical notes, they have trouble identifying which ones are higher in pitch. This experiment gives them the opportunity to explore what pitch is.

Objectives

- To understand the concept of pitch.
- To make and then test predictions.

Student Instruction

Explain the difference between volume and pitch. Demonstrate higher and lower volumes, using louder and softer sounds. Then demonstrate different pitches. This could be done with a musical instrument such as a piano or recorder, by singing different notes, or by using examples from the animal kingdom. For example, a mouse makes a high-pitched squeak while a lion has a low-pitched roar. Point out that these two animals also have different volumes because a lion's roar is louder than a mouse's squeak.

If you are going to have students fill the bottles themselves, introduce the funnel, what it is used for, and how to use it.

Center Preparation

Materials: 3 identical glass bottles, 12-16 ounce (360-500 mL) size; 1 metal teaspoon (5 mL); water; pitcher; 1 funnel; a 12" (30 cm) ruler; bath towel

Directions: Cover the table in the center with a bath towel. This helps absorb the spills and keeps the glass bottles from slipping off the table. Provide a metal teaspoon and three identical bottles from juice or soft drinks with lids. Label them *A, B*, and *C*. Pour water into each bottle, making sure there are different amounts in each. For younger students, fill the bottles ahead of time, and put on the lids to minimize spills. If you are going to have students fill the bottles, you will need a funnel and an easy-to-use pitcher.

Follow-Up Activities

Have students predict how the size and shape of a bottle will affect its pitch. Get several bottles and jars of different sizes, and allow students to try them out. Note that there are many variables in this follow-up experiment, so the results are likely to be different from what you would expect. In other words, this is not a controlled experiment. However, this type of follow-up still helps reinforce the basic concepts and motivates students toward doing their own explorations.

Relate the partially filled bottles to a flute, recorder, or clarinet. As you close more of the holes on these instruments, you effectively make the air column longer. This is analogous to taking water out of the bottles to achieve a lower pitch.

Name: _____ Date: _____

Perfect Pitch

Lab Worksheet — Level A

Ask Yourself

How can I change the pitch of a sound?

What You Need

_____ 3 glass bottles

_____ Water

_____ 1 metal spoon

What You Do

Use **Bottle A** and **Bottle B**.

_____ 1. Tap each bottle with the spoon.

_____ 2. Which has a lower pitch? _____ Bottle A _____ Bottle B

_____ 3. Which one has more air? _____ Bottle A _____ Bottle B

Use **Bottle A** and **Bottle C**.

_____ 4. Which has more air? _____ Bottle A _____ Bottle C

_____ 5. Predict: Which do you think has a lower pitch?
_____ Bottle A _____ Bottle C

_____ 6. Tap each bottle with the spoon.

_____ 7. Which has a lower pitch? _____ Bottle A _____ Bottle C

Use **Bottle B** and **Bottle C**.

_____ 8. Which has more air? _____ Bottle B _____ Bottle C

_____ 9. Predict: Which do you think has a lower pitch?
_____ Bottle B _____ Bottle C

_____ 10. Tap each bottle with the spoon.

_____ 11. Which has a lower pitch? _____ Bottle B _____ Bottle C

What You Learned

Does a bottle with more air have a higher or lower pitch? _____

Name: _____ Date: _____

Perfect Pitch

Lab Worksheet — Level B

Ask Yourself

How can I change the pitch of the sound made by tapping a bottle with a spoon?

_____

What You Need

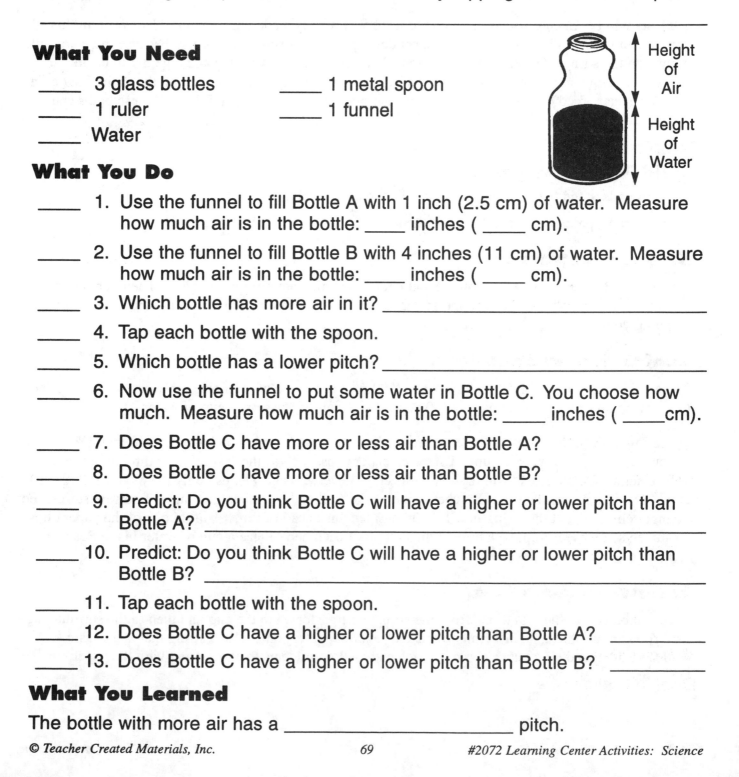

Height of Air

Height of Water

_____ 3 glass bottles   _____ 1 metal spoon

_____ 1 ruler   _____ 1 funnel

_____ Water

What You Do

_____ 1. Use the funnel to fill Bottle A with 1 inch (2.5 cm) of water. Measure how much air is in the bottle: _____ inches (_____ cm).

_____ 2. Use the funnel to fill Bottle B with 4 inches (11 cm) of water. Measure how much air is in the bottle: _____ inches (_____ cm).

_____ 3. Which bottle has more air in it? _____

_____ 4. Tap each bottle with the spoon.

_____ 5. Which bottle has a lower pitch? _____

_____ 6. Now use the funnel to put some water in Bottle C. You choose how much. Measure how much air is in the bottle: _____ inches (_____cm).

_____ 7. Does Bottle C have more or less air than Bottle A?

_____ 8. Does Bottle C have more or less air than Bottle B?

_____ 9. Predict: Do you think Bottle C will have a higher or lower pitch than Bottle A? _____

_____ 10. Predict: Do you think Bottle C will have a higher or lower pitch than Bottle B? _____

_____ 11. Tap each bottle with the spoon.

_____ 12. Does Bottle C have a higher or lower pitch than Bottle A? _____

_____ 13. Does Bottle C have a higher or lower pitch than Bottle B? _____

What You Learned

The bottle with more air has a _____ pitch.

Play It Loudly

Background

The volume of a sound is how loud or soft it is. In scientific terms, volume is how much energy the vibrations have. Pitch, on the other hand, is how fast or slow the vibrations are. In this activity, students will experiment with volume by adding a sound box, or resonant cavity. This is essentially equivalent to the wooden body of a violin.

Students will be making sound in much the same way as it is made with a violin. However, in this experiment they will be running their fingers down pieces of string. This works because there are little bumps on the string. These bumps appeared when many strands were twisted together to create the string. Your fingers bounce over the bumps and cause the vibrations. The hair on the violin bow comes from a special breed of horse that has larger-than-normal barbs on their tail hairs. These barbs cause the vibrations.

Objectives

- To understand the concept of volume as it relates to sound.
- To make predictions, and then test them.

Student Instruction

Explain the difference between volume and pitch. Demonstrate different pitches. Then demonstrate higher and lower volumes (louder and softer sounds). This could be done with a radio or simply by clapping your hands.

Center Preparation

Materials: 8 ounce (250 mL) and 16 ounce (500 mL) cups, one of each size for every student; 75 feet (22.5 m) of string; 4 paper clips; 12" (30 cm) ruler; 1 pair of scissors; a cup of water

Directions: The exact sizes of the cups are not important, as long as you have two different sizes. Use either waxed paper or plastic cups. Uncoated paper cups, such as those sold for bathroom use, are not stiff enough. For students using Lab Worksheet — Level A (page 71), use only the 8 ounce (250 mL) cups. The string must be thin. Butcher twine works well and is available at many hardware stores. For younger children, cut the string into 12" (30 cm) lengths ahead of time. Unfold one of the paper clips so students can use it to poke a hole in the bottom of each cup. Place a cup of water in the Science Center so students can wet their fingers.

Follow-Up Activities

In this experiment, the vibrations from the string are transferred to the cup and then to the surrounding air. You can use the same principle to make a paper cup telephone. Use a string that is at least 4' (1.2 m) long and tie a paper cup onto each end. Allow students to experiment with the paper cup telephone.

Name: _____ Date: _____

Play It Loudly

Lab Worksheet — Level A

Ask Yourself

What is the body of a violin for?

What You Need

____ 2 pieces of string   ____ 1 paper cup

____ 3 paper clips   ____ 1 cup of water

What You Do

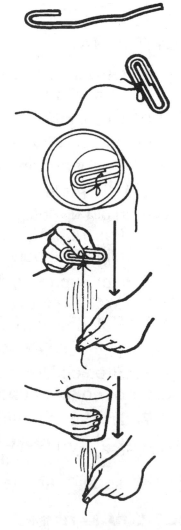

____ 1. Untwist one paper clip. Use it to poke a hole in the bottom of the cup. Do not use this paper clip again.

____ 2. Tie a paper clip to one end of each string.

____ 3. Put one string through the hole in the cup. The paper clip tied onto the end of the string should be inside the cup.

____ 4. Hold up the string without the cup by the paper clip. Get your finger tips wet. Squeeze the string between your finger tips near the paper clip. Pull down on the string with your finger tips. You should hear a sound.

____ 5. Hold up the cup with the string hanging down. Get your fingers wet. Squeeze the string between your finger tips near the cup. Pull down on the string with your fingers tips. You should hear another sound.

What You Learned

Which sound was louder? _____ with the cup _____ without the cup

Name: _____ Date: _____

Play It Loudly

Lab Worksheet — Level B

Ask Yourself

What is the body of a violin for?_____

What You Need

_____ String

_____ 4 paper clips

_____ 1 small paper cup

_____ 1 large paper cup

_____ 1 ruler

_____ 1 pair of scissors

_____ Water

What You Do

_____ 1. Untwist one paper clip. Use it to poke a hole in the bottom of each cup. Do not use this paper clip again.

_____ 2. Cut 3 pieces of string, each 12 inches (30 cm) long. Tie a paper clip to one end of each string.

_____ 3. Put one string through the hole in each cup. The paper clips should be inside the cups.

_____ 4. Hold up the string without the cup by the paper clip. Get your finger tips wet. Squeeze the string between your finger tips near the paper clip. Pull down on the string. You should hear a sound.

_____ 5. Hold up the small cup with the string hanging down. Get your fingers wet. Squeeze the string between your finger tips near the small cup. Pull down on the string with your fingers tips. Is this sound louder or softer than the first sound? _____

_____ 6. Predict: Do you think the string with the large cup will make a louder or softer sound than the one with the small cup? _____

_____ 7. Hold up the large cup with the string hanging down. Get your fingers wet. Squeeze the string between your finger tips near the large cup. Pull down on the string with your finger tips. Is this sound louder or softer than the one made with the small cup?

What You Learned

The cup is like the body of a violin in that it helps to _____

_____.

Prancing Pepper

Background

If you slowly and carefully fill a glass with water, you can actually put in so much that the water is higher than the top of the glass. The surface tension of the water keeps it from spilling. Surface tension tends to keep a liquid together. If we put a few drops of oil on top of water, they will stay there in a blob and not mix into the water. If we put a few drops of detergent on top of water, they will also remain there in a blob. The blob of detergent, however, flattens out. It has to spread sideways as it flattens. If anything happens to be floating on the surface of the water, it will get pushed aside by the spreading detergent.

Objectives

- To introduce the idea that liquids behave differently, in this case because of surface tension.
- To document observations using a sketch or diagram.

Student Instruction

Talk about different kinds of liquids and the properties they have: how they smell, taste, and feel; how thick they are; etc. Demonstrate how some liquids mix together and others do not. Using liquids of different colors is a dramatic way to show this. For example, pour cooking oil into water with red food color in it. **Helpful Hint:** Yellow food color can be added to the cooking oil to make it easier to see.

Center Preparation

Materials: 1 bowl or saucer, about 5" (13 cm) wide and 1-2" (2.5-5 cm) deep; pepper shaker with black pepper; liquid dish detergent; empty, clean liquid dish detergent bottle; cooking oil; water; plastic pitcher or small plastic bottle; paper towels

Directions: The bowl or saucer can be made from plastic. Purchase liquid dish detergent that comes in a squeeze bottle so students will be able to add just a drop or two. Save an empty liquid detergent bottle, rinse and dry it well, then put some oil in it. This way students will also be able to squeeze out just a drop or two of oil. Use a permanent marker to label the bottle of oil. As an alternative to using liquid detergent bottles, pour the detergent and oil into separate plastic cups. Students can use separate eye droppers to add these liquids to the water in the bowl.

The water should be in a plastic pitcher or small plastic bottle so students can easily pour it. After the experiment, students should dump the contents of the bowl or saucer into a sink or bucket. Have them wipe the bowl with a paper towel to remove any pepper, oil, or detergent that may be stuck to the sides.

Follow-Up Activities

Another example of the differences between oil and water can be dramatically demonstrated with a feather. Dip the feather in water, and show your class that the feather is not damaged and barely appears to be wet. Now create an oil spill by pouring some cooking oil on top of the water. Dip the feather in again, and they will see that the oil adheres well to the feather. Use this to discuss the implications of oil spills on aquatic birds.

Name: _____ Date: _____

Prancing Pepper

Lab Worksheet — Level A

Ask Yourself

Do oil and soap act the same way when they are put in water?

What You Need

_____ 1 bowl   _____ Oil

_____ Pepper   _____ Soap

_____ Water

What You Do

_____ 1. Pour water into the bowl until it is half full.

_____ 2. Sprinkle a little pepper on top of the water in the bowl.

_____ 3. Look at the cup of water with the pepper in it. Use the back of this paper to draw a sketch of what you see. Label this picture with the letter **A.**

_____ 4. Add 1-2 drops of oil to the water.

_____ 5. Look at the oil in the cup of water. Use the back of this paper to draw a sketch of what you see. Label this picture with the letter **B.**

_____ 6. Add 1-2 drops of soap to the water.

_____ 7. Look at the soap in the cup of water. Use the back of this paper to draw a sketch of what you see. Label this picture with the letter **C.**

What You Learned

What happened when you added the oil?

_____

What happened when you added the soap? _____

_____

Name: _____ Date: _____

Prancing Pepper

Lab Worksheet — Level B

Ask Yourself

How will oil and soap act differently when they are put in water? _____

_____

_____

What You Need

_____ 1 bowl   _____ Soap

_____ Oil   _____ Water

_____ Pepper

What You Do

_____ 1. Pour water into the bowl until it is half full.

_____ 2. Sprinkle a little pepper on top of the water in the bowl.

_____ 3. Look at the cup of water with the pepper in it. Use the back of this paper to draw a diagram of what you see. Write the title "Diagram A" above this picture. Label the water and pepper.

_____ 4. Add 1-2 drops of oil to the water.

_____ 5. Look at the oil in the cup of water. Use the back of this paper to draw a diagram of what you see. Write the title "Diagram B" above this picture. Label the water, pepper, and oil.

_____ 6. Add 1-2 drops of soap to the water.

_____ 7. Look at the soap in the cup of water. Use the back of this paper to draw a diagram of what you see. Write the title "Diagram C" above this picture. Label the water, pepper, oil, and soap.

What You Learned

How did the oil react differently than the soap when added to the water?_____

_____

_____

Pretty Pennies

Background

To make pennies nice and shiny, an acid is required. Vinegar is a mild acid but it is not strong enough to clean the pennies. However, the acid made by adding salt to the vinegar is. Students can try physical means to clean the pennies like scrubbing them. They should find that scrubbing is ineffective. However, a quick dip in the acid bath makes the pennies go through a magical change.

Objectives

- To introduce the idea of a chemical reaction.

- To introduce the use of a control as a means of evaluating the results of the experiment.

Student Instruction

Warning: This experiment is safe; however, vinegar will sting if it gets into the eyes or cuts. Be sure to follow these two safety precautions: (1) Have students wear safety goggles, and (2) have them put the pennies into the solutions using a clothespin.

Center Preparation

Materials: 1 clothespin; paper cups, 3-ounce (90 mL) size, 3 per student; dirty pennies; white vinegar; water; salt; bath towel

Directions: Buy a large bottle of white vinegar and a box of table salt at a grocery store. Save two empty squeeze bottles such as those used for dish washing detergent or shampoo. Be sure to rinse them thoroughly. Label one bottle *Water* and the other *Vinegar*. Fill each bottle with the appropriate liquid. Using the squeeze bottles will make it easier for students to prepare the experiment without spilling or splashing. For younger students, you may prefer to have the cups already filled with the proper chemicals. These chemicals can be used over and over so you may wish to store them in baby food jars or other containers with lids. Since this is a chemistry experiment, students should be required to wear safety goggles. If students work with a partner, both should wear goggles. You will also need three small paper cups per student, one teaspoon (plastic or metal), and one clothespin. Ask each student to bring 2-3 old pennies, the dirtier the better, or provide a supply of these yourself. **Helpful Hint:** You can get a roll of pennies at a local bank. Cover the work surface with a bath towel to soak up spills.

Follow-Up Activities

Have students try other acids, such as lemon juice or cola, to see which ones will clean the pennies.

Provide other coins for students to experiment with and allow them to discover that this method of cleaning only works for pennies because they are made from copper.

Name: _____ Date: _____

Pretty Pennies

Lab Worksheet — Level A

Ask Yourself

How can I clean dirty pennies?

What You Need

_____ safety goggles

_____ 2 dirty pennies

_____ 1 cup of water

_____ 1 cup of vinegar

_____ 1 cup of vinegar mixed with salt

_____ 1 clothespin

_____ 1 paper towel

What You Do

_____ 1. Put on your safety goggles.

_____ 2. Dip the paper towel in the water to get it wet.

_____ 3. Try to clean one of the pennies using the wet paper towel.

_____ 4. Write what happened in the chart on page 78.

_____ 5. Hold the penny using the clothespin.

_____ 6. Dip the penny in the cup of water.

_____ 7. Write what happened in the chart on page 78.

_____ 8. Dip the penny in the cup of vinegar.

_____ 9. Write what happened in the chart on page 78.

_____ 10. Dip the penny in the cup of vinegar and salt.

_____ 11. Write what happened on the chart on page 78.

Name: _____ Date: _____

Pretty Pennies (cont.)

Lab Worksheet — Level A (cont.)

Try This	Did the first penny get clean?		Did the second penny get clean?	
	Yes	No	Yes	No
Wash with paper towel				
Dip in water				
Dip in vinegar				
Dip in vinegar and salt				

What You Learned

What is the best way to clean a dirty penny?

_____ With water

_____ With vinegar

_____ With vinegar and salt

Name: _____ Date: _____

Pretty Pennies
Lab Worksheet — Level B

Ask Yourself

How can I clean dirty pennies? _____

_____

What You Need

____ 3 small paper cups

____ Vinegar

____ 1 teaspoon (5 mL)

____ Water

____ 1 clothespin

____ Salt

____ 2 dirty pennies

____ 1 paper towel

____ Safety goggles

____ Pen or marker

What You Do

____ 1. Mark your three cups: **W** for water, **V** for vinegar, and **V + S** for vinegar and salt.

____ 2. Put on your safety goggles.

____ 3. Fill the **W** cup half way with water.

____ 4. Fill the **V** and **V + S** cups half way with vinegar.

____ 5. Add 1 teaspoon (5 mL) of salt to the **V + S** cup and stir.

____ 6. Predict: Do you think the penny will get clean when you dip it into the **W** cup? ____ Yes   ____ No

____ 7. Hold one penny using the clothespin.

____ 8. Dip the penny in the **W** cup.

____ 9. Did the penny get clean? Write what happened in the chart on page 80.

____ 10. Predict: Do you think the penny will get clean when you dip it into the **V** cup? ____ Yes   ____ No

____ 11. Dip the penny in the **V** cup.

____ 12. Did the penny get clean? Write what happened in the chart on page 80.

____ 13. Predict: Do you think the penny will get clean when you dip it into the **V + S** cup? ____ Yes   ____ No

____ 14. Dip the penny in the **V + S** cup.

____ 15. Did the penny get clean? Write what happened in the chart on page 80.

____ 16. Repeat steps 7, 8, 9, 11, 12, 14, and 15 for another penny. Write the results on the next page.

Name: _____   Date: _____

Pretty Pennies *(cont.)*

Lab Worksheet — Level B *(cont.)*

Try This	Did the first penny get clean?		Did the second penny get clean?	
	Yes	No	Yes	No
Dip in water **(W).**				
Dip in vinegar **(V).**				
Dip in vinegar and salt **(V + S).**				

What You Learned

Did you get the same results for both pennies? If not, how were they different?

_____

_____

Which type of liquid cleaned the pennies best?

_____

_____

Why does one clear liquid clean pennies better than another clear liquid?

_____

_____

_____